No Such Dvsn

Eclipse: Side A

Eclipse, Volume 1

Sakari Lacross

Published by Sakari Lacross, 2024.

ECLIPSE: SIDE A

First edition. August 3, 2024.

ISBN: 979-8230050254

Written by Sakari Lacross.

Table of Contents

Your body's crying, instead of your eyes

Like it's that easy, for everything to come out

And I know you'd rather this

Legs around my neck, you'd rather this

Questions about how you feel

You'd rather I...

~ Sakari

You're giving me what I asked for

So what more could I ask for

If I thought of anything

Could I ask this of you too

Lying in my bed, with your chest covered

Sideways we face each other

~ Sakari

One day it'll be us

And you'll be into me

You'll give into me

And I'll be inside of you

~ Sakari

No one really understands

That when she lets you inside

She's really trusting you

When her legs wrap around you

She's really trusting you

~ Sakari

Hope you aren't telling yourself

That you could do better.

You were amazing.

The way you shivered on top of me...

The way you pulled back, just in time...

You were amazing.

~ Sakari

Why All Of It Matters

Your body and its current

I'm asking you to crash into me

I'll survive

Looking for you, in the seas around me

~ Sakari

It's like it doesn't make sense

And I won't make sense of it

As a poet, what do I really say

With how you look, I'm sure everything,

Has already been said

~ Sakari

Buttons with butterflies instead

You have the face of a kitten

I wish this was in an envelope instead

A 4 page love letter, from front to back

~ Sakari

Wishing is all I can do

Waterfalls from Nature's Valley, you must bathe to

Because I can't find a sprinkle of flaws upon you

Through desert sands, my eyes drag

Rose petals that fall out, onto your lap

~ Sakari

From this same love letter, hopefully I grab

Ahold of your hand in spirit

A spiritual touch, to your heart

~ Sakari

The Rush

The way we both decide

What we go through next

You just got off your period

So nothing's unusual next

~ Sakari

If only it mattered

What came off first

I'd be picky

Your shorts would go

And with only your shirt on

Because I refuse this wait

You climb on top of me

In the air, we refuse this wait

~ Sakari

I'm right in front of you

So it's not autocorrect

But I get it

We've never done this

So I don't expect

Automatic

Though you lean in so close

It feels like it could happen

A slight smirk because you're shy

While your hands...are automatic

~ Sakari

Less revealing, and you still get me like this

So much of my imagination, and you still get me

The only way I see us, we're lying down like this

Only questions until I see you again

You're moving around my room, like this

~ Sakari

And with your batteries dead again

It's up to me

I didn't prepare

So it's lip service, instead

~ Sakari

Every First Morning

Sitting in the sun with you...

Pulling away from the scenery...

Taking away from nothing with you...

Giving into something with you...

~ Sakari

To keep you always naked in my bed

Is the goal

Mirrors that show you off in my room

Making you self-absorbed

I'm gone and you're alone

I'll be back after my tour

~ Sakari

Perfect like AI...

Unbelievable like AI...

Put together like AI...

In my hands like AI...

~ Sakari

And I hope your music's still playing

I hope we don't have to stop

I hope we're not being too loud

I hope your legs continue to shake

***

Crossing the day away

***

I hope this is what I can feel tomorrow

I hope you sex me more than once

I hope it's up to me when I can see you again

I hope it's just you and me, from morning until lunch

***

Crossing the day away

~ Sakari

Catch up while I slow down for you

I'm doing too much with too many girls

My heart's been single for a while now

These girls, these girls

Get me through a lot

Sometimes I want them all

All these feelings I box

In a perfect world, in a perfect world

~ Sakari

All Of It Isn't Dread

Fallen angels don't get to hold hearts

We're used to that

We admire from a distance, and hope our wings

Bring us closure

~ Sakari

Tell me bye and I'll understand

I missed you as soon as I woke up and realized

You weren't in the same bed as me

~ Sakari

Rhythm & U

Splashes over the bed

Where else can you roll over to

We can switch places

I'll lie in your splash

And you can take refuge

On top of me

~ Sakari

He plays with your heart

But leaves your body on rest

Can this be reset

With you in a brand new bed

~ Sakari

It's slow motion at first

The way we text and talk

You're his at first

Questions about this, the more we talk

~ Sakari

All of my attention, you have

All of my attention, can I have the hurt you hold

Within a safe, I'll place it

And in my room number, you'll be safe

Like catching butterflies for the night

I'll conceal you

Knowing you'll glow when the lights shut out

This is how you'll heal

~ Sakari

When it's you who's sleep next to me

I sleep too

Rolling over in a haze

Just to hold you

Cuffing you

As if you'll roll away

Coiled to you...

Coiled to you...

~ Sakari

Medium Piece

I wanna catch you on my tongue and surprise all your friends

I know you'll hint to what happen on your social media

To watch your mood change over night

I know you'll hint to what happen on your social media

~ Sakari

The way we rotate

We spin in cycles

Neither can let the other take control

It's not about trust, it's pure consumption

~ Sakari

Tonight is an embrace session

You're the only existing appointment

Caught up by recent "no-shows"

Hopefully, this evening changes

***

Lighted shades so the night can see

Hearts so full that get emptied

Vases of valued chemistry

We're equivalent to each other, like alchemy

~ Sakari

Your river calls unknown

Hopefully it's in private, your water flows

Like I'm the lucky one, I swear I know

The unknown one, to this I know

~ Sakari

Like sex in a dream

It feels unrealistic

Because it's you who's here

But I'm dreading waking up

Because you feel just as I imagined

Like we're touring without protection

***

There's barely any guidance

This feels like instinct

And instead of voicing our commands

We're reacting to everything

Shaking and jerking to everything

Careful not to finish before the other

~ Sakari

More Of This

The sun will not complete its rise

Only its set

It's a beautiful yet sad sight

~ Sakari

With my hands reaching for the night

A beautiful response was sent

The universe gave me a friend

A friend that also reached for the night

And through universes, I wanted to send

Her flowers, a rose for every day

We thread dimensions within both domains

I close my eyes and ask for an expansion

So that both of our worlds touch

And I'm able to walk a single flower to her

I close my eyes and ask for an expansion

We thread dimensions within both domains

~ Sakari

You're taking up too many notes in my phone

I start to tell myself there's no such thing

When it's only this girl, I stay up for

Different time zones completely

My night is her day

~ Sakari

For the love of water away from land...

Sky water that has nowhere else to go...

Let's fall like the rain

Nothing else included...

~ Sakari

We can't worry about tomorrow

I can't keep being scared

There's this fear that I'll run you off

There's this fear that I'm liking you too much

~ Sakari

Like Any Other Night

Your muscles are tight, if I had to guess

Your body's so tight, can there be, a given match-up

A struggle to get through, I only hope so

An effort to get out, I only hope so

~ Sakari

You're only a toss over away

Your hair stretches to the middle

If only your body would get this same courage

We could get through this restless night

~ Sakari

This view, if only...

Your head tilted back, if only...

Because you're halfway off the bed, if only...

Nearing the second floor window, inside a large cabin, if only...

~ Sakari

Triple-doubles throughout the entire night

It's been all year I've been wanting this

And time has no patience, so we're going through this

And so often, I feel you clenching

You're letting go this entire year as well

~ Sakari

She'd train me to become her tongue devil

I'd deliver and leave never

Thinking alone and without the other

We'd get to masturbating and responding to instant messages

~ Sakari

Becoming Envy, Becoming Darkness

A Shadow's Wheel

Do I sound good coming from your mind

How does my voice hold up in your head

Spell it out to me

I'm still lost

~ Sakari

Today melts in my palm

Just one long rift that runs together

Your feelings manipulate me

I'm on your vertigo ride

~ Sakari

I came to you when these words traveled

Is it true

How long has he had you

~ Sakari

Walking away means goodbye

Walk away from him instead of me

This time

~ Sakari

Like a teenager all over again

I'm watching him hold your hand

~ Sakari

Know that my own art hurts me

With a false inspiration of you

You wear black so well

Do the shadows know you too

~ Sakari

Eyes Of Envy

He's got his hands on you

I wish I was the one touching you

With fingers as deep

As the words I write about you

~ Sakari

All I can teach you

Is how to lust with heartbreak

To embody what you hate

~ Sakari

You never have to tell me

When you sneak around

I still want you

~ Sakari

The easiest way to my heart

Is you

Cheating is small

You not coming back is a calamity

~ Sakari

I bet he won't pick you up when you're down

I bet he won't stay consistent

You feel like the weed I smoke

I'm dosing off inhaling you

~ Sakari

The problem is I move on too fast

There's always someone I want

What's there to think about

Your body seems great for me

~ Sakari

And all the while I can't take it

I can't take not catching you during a sunset

In the slightest chance I have you

I won't have to cry as much

~ Sakari

Imagine us finishing

At the same time

Oh how I love

Our 69's

~ Sakari

Heartbroken Hellraiser

You would lose your memory every day

But you were my girlfriend

Every day, I would reintroduce myself to you

Us living together, was all I could prove

Yet somehow, your heart told me to stay

Like you, I wanted to keep your memory

~ Sakari

We were forced to start over love

On a daily basis

I never blamed you or your seizures

For any of this

~ Sakari

I touch your stomach a lot

I wish our baby was still in there

~ Sakari

Some things they can't see

No longer dealing with the police

I know my mother still judges me

~ Sakari

When I was supporting your drug habit

We were so close, dad

But for over a decade

I've been a man without you

Wishing I was in high school

And you would come get me without notice

~ Sakari

I'm used to the inner war

Whatever circle we thought we had

Has been broken

~ Sakari

I might not ever give up the weed

Tossing and turning throughout the night

This shit gives me some form of sleep

~ Sakari

How many people did I hurt for you, mother

Both mentally and physically

But you always needed me war ready

~ Sakari

The last time we talked

You mocked that my children were deceased

I mocked about your mother being six feet

Yeah, dad, there's not too much more talking we can do

~ Sakari

I can't relate to his pain

He lost his mother at thirteen

So I was born

Without any grandparents

~ Sakari

Everything Not To Ignore Her

Mind Of Illusion

I let my heart down

You can have it while my life's in reverse

~ Sakari

Feel like I need love, but I don't know why.

A child of Greed and Lust

I'm Envy

~ Sakari

Every time I've moved on

I was forced to

You don't want me

~ Sakari

It's only one girl

Who ever kept me out of trouble

Bet I run into

Whatever new dude, she keeps out of trouble

~ Sakari

I wish I had a hole somewhere else

Besides my chest

Wish I bled somewhere else

Besides my heart

~ Sakari

I was all alone

When they took the other inmates

Out my cell

~ Sakari

Seems like every girl is taken nowadays

"Can I talk to you now?"

Is said a lot, nowadays

~ Sakari

My life's been hit with invisible cleavers

Do you still find interest

In dismantled me

~ Sakari

You ever want someone

To not really know you

Even though

They already know you

~ Sakari

She's not mine, but I wanna be near her

Placing her in the back of my mind, I can never tell her

~ Sakari

Heart Of Chaos

My heart hurts

But my mind is dark

It's contracted to me

This darkness

~ Sakari

We go through everything but good times

These bad times used to take up my schedule

~ Sakari

I need you to hold my hand

As the shadows drain me

~ Sakari

Don't miss out!

Visit the website below and you can sign up to receive emails whenever Sakari Lacross publishes a new book. There's no charge and no obligation.

https://books2read.com/r/B-A-GXQL-MMGBE

BOOKS 2 READ

Connecting independent readers to independent writers.

Did you love *Eclipse: Side A*? Then you should read *Burn Brothers*[1] by Sakari Lacross!

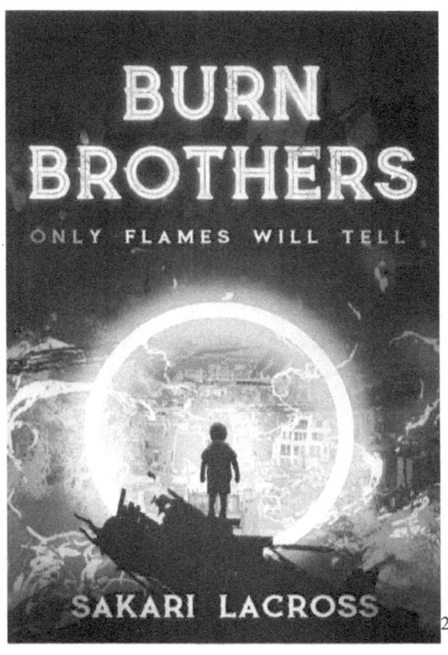

[2]

Jayk, a super-powered being with the ability to manifest and manipulate fire, has tried to keep his powers a secret. He has tried to live a normal life, living amongst mortals as he always intended. However, the one thing that he has run from, has finally caught up to him. A part of his past that could jepardize his future if it isn't stopped...his younger brother.

1. https://books2read.com/u/bWG2Q7

2. https://books2read.com/u/bWG2Q7

Also by Sakari Lacross

A Dawn Breaking Romance

Romance Dawn

Beyond Dawn

A Final World

Rising Tides

Don't End Up Consumed

Don't End Up Consumed 2

Belonging

I Hope I Belong

I Hope I Belong Too

Eclipse

Eclipse: Side A

Eclipse Side B

Perfect Gentleman
Perfect Gentleman

Simp Undying
I Simp For You
I Simp For You Too
Another Reason To Simp

Soft Hardcover
New Love Plus(+)

Sunset Szn
Sunset Szn
Sunset SZN 2
Sunset SZN 3

The Last Witch
The Last Witch: Book 1
The Last Witch: Book 2

This Is For Her

Someone Like You

Someone Like You Too

Someone Else Like You

Threads

Threads

Standalone

The Legend Of Krampus

Deeper Than Magic

A Place Inside My Castle

Luminary

Loyalist To The Moon

Thoughts & Memories

Ideas & Reality

Vines & Beauty

V For Her

Playing With Skeletons

About the Author

Sakari Lacross was born February 5th, 1994, in Cleveland Ohio. Spending most of his childhood being raised in Flint Michigan, Sakari's mother moved him and his family to Arizona when he was 15. Sakari has been writing since he was nine years old, competing in his school's poetry contest and bimonthly writing events. Discovering all his true potential to write during his years he went to linden charter academy, Sakari won his first local poetry contest at Sam Garcia Western Avenue Library, located in Avondale Arizona. Sakari then published his first poetry collection, titled, PTSD.

www.ingramcontent.com/pod-product-compliance
Lightning Source LLC
LaVergne TN
LVHW040943150826
845672LV00002B/511

* 9 7 9 8 2 3 0 0 5 0 2 5 4 *